Illustrated by Colorado Kids

Written by Natalie Myers

Colorado Kids Create, Inc. encourages artistic expression in youth and empowers Colorado teachers.

Dedicated to everyone who has helped this project over the past ten years but especially Lisa and Steve Steele for their consistent devotion to getting art supplies to needy classrooms in our state!

Join in the fun of the annual Colorado Kids Create drawing contest and win great prizes at:

coloradokidscreate.org

Purchase other Colorado Kids Create books and e-books on Amazon.
Positive reviews are important, please leave one.
Reach us at coloradokidscreate@gmail.com

Copyright 2022 by Colorado Kids Create, Inc.
All rights reserved. This book or any portion thereof may not be reproduced or used in any manner whatsoever without the express written permission of the publisher except for the use of brief quotations in a book review.

What can you do to care for Colorado?

Once upon a fleeting time, the Colorado

Tourism Office partnered with a conservation

organization called Leave No Trace. They came

up with 7 Care for Colorado principles.

They decided more people needed to know these

practices to protect Colorado's natural resources.

What are natural resources?

Watch the video and learn

the Care for Colorado song

sung by Micah Morris on the

Colorado Tourism website.

"Care for Colorado.

It's the only one we've got.

Respect the place, leave no trace.

It sure would help a lot!

Here is how we do it: #1 Know Before You Go!

And go where fewer people go.

And keep yourself hydrated.

Disposables are over-rated.

#2 Stick to the Trails!

The Rocky Mountains don't have rails.

A new path may seem fun,

but it causes lots of erosion.

#3 Leave It As You Found It!

The flowers and the trees.

We don't need to know

who you dated in 1983.

Care for Colorado.

It's the only one we've got.

#4 Trash the Trash!

Do we really need to write

a clever lyric about putting your

trash in the trash can?

And keep in mind

you'd hate to find,

a domestic critter's leave-behind.

#5 Be Careful with Fire!

Make sure they are out and won't grow higher.

Even a little cigarette haze

could cause a major forest blaze.

#6 Keep Wildlife Wild!

They may be cuddly and cute

24

But give them food and I'm telling

you, Dude, best not get them riled.

#7 Share Our Trails and Parks

in every kind of weather!

Be respectful of other's space.

We're all in this together.

Care for Colorado

It's the only one we've got.

Respect the place, leave no trace.

And thank you, you really helped a lot!"

Leave No Trace Seven Principles © 1999 by the Leave No Trace Center for Outdoor Ethics: www.LNT.org

Learn more by visiting https://www.colorado.com/CareForColorado and https://oedit.colorado.gov/colorado-tourism-office

Fun Facts to Know

Colorado has 39,000 marked trails

and 13,000 designated campsites!

By sticking to these areas and camping at least

200 feet from lakes, rivers, and streams,

you're helping natural areas stay natural.

State and Federal agencies protect 42% of

Colorado's majestic landscape. There are 750

different species of wildflowers.

They live forever in a photo.

Carving or hacking plants and trees may kill them.

Wash yourself, dog, or whatever needs cleaning

at least 200 feet from waterways and use

biodegradable soap. Fish don't enjoy bubble baths!

When putting out a fire, water it until

you can handle the embers.

Never leave a fire burning unattended.

Always check for local fire restrictions.

Feeding wild animals can alter natural behaviors,

exposing them to predators or even death.

It is important to yield to the uphill

hiker or biker-they need momentum.

Silence your phone before

stepping into nature and

speak softly without

using the speaker function.

Or better yet, just

watch and listen

to all the

landscape has to offer.

Above all, remember this,

Colorado kids don't destroy.

Colorado Kids Create!!

Take me where the wildflowers grow

Thank You to All Colorado Kids Create Illustrators and Teachers!!
Cover- Clara Seo 12, Colorado Springs   Title Page- Desiree Martinez 15, Pueblo

Pg. 1 Kalie Champlain 15, Pueblo
2. Nora Myers 9, Evans
3. Ashton Lower 10, Loveland
4. Rebecca Feng 9, Thornton
5. Avalon Parlin 13, Evans
6. Sophie Ham 13, Grand Junction
7. Nataly Pham 12, Thornton
8. Gabriella Hagedorn 13, Bellvue
9. Rian Kim 8, Fort Collins
10. Luca Williford 9, Crested Butte
11. Norah Mackey 9, Westminster
12. Harika Shankar 18, Fort Collins
13. Enora Zhang 10, Windsor
14. Ayanna Bailey 10, Fort Collins
15. Elorah Valdez 14, Pueblo
16. Delilah Belarde 18, Pueblo
17. Lux Ross 9, Castle Rock
18. Aralyn Burghelea 9, Fort Collins
19. Gisele Gates 13, Windsor
20. Lucas Gilmore 7, Denver
21. Anabelle Remakus 9, Fort Collins
22. Asher Sanders 6, Fort Collins
23. Anelise Medina 17, Pueblo
23. Owen Myers 7, Evans
25. Kayci Huelskamp 12, Flagler
26. Andon Schleich 13, Grand Junction
27. Zoie Pelc 10, Fort Collins
28. Nicole Solano 18, Pueblo
29. Kylee McLaughlin 13, Grand Junction
31. Monika Shankar 13, Fort Collins
32. Isley Williams 8, Fort Collins
33. Elizabeth Herzog 17, Pueblo
34. Emily Sparks 13, Grand Junction
35. Anna Garnett 15, Pueblo
36. Kylee Mclaughlin 13, Grand Junction
37. Darina Tsuber 11, Thornton
38. Kyleigh Lee 11, Aurora
39. Katy Mallory 7, Fort Collins
40. Jalaigh Nygaard 10, Fort Collins
41. Charlotte Ables 8, Fort Collins
42. Rebecca Johnson 12, Fort Collins
43. Elle Benedetto 16, Pueblo
44. Lakshmi Aneesh 6, Fort Collins
45. Ali Weisheit 10, Castlerock
46. Julianna Cardona 17, Pueblo
47. Emilia Varvanuk 12, Thornton
48. Emma Kim 11, Aurora
49. Evan Doyun Lee 9, Highlands Ranch
50. Taylor Umberger 13, Grand Junction

Ingram Content Group UK Ltd.
Milton Keynes UK
UKHW051908260423
420851UK00002B/10